# BACKSTAGE BERLIN

RÜCKANSICHTEN DER HAUPTSTADT | A LOOK BEHIND THE SCENES

**MARKUS C. HUREK**

Prestel

Munich · Berlin · London · New York

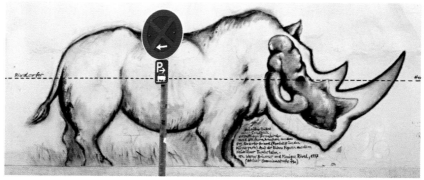

**Saltykowstraße, Neukölln**

»Die Schönheit der Stadt zeigt sich auf den **zweiten** Blick«

SWISS Magazine, Mai 2003

»You have to look twice to discover the beauty of the city«

Natürlich kennen Sie den Reichstag, das Brandenburger Tor, Klaus Wowereit und Knut. »Sehn Se dit is Berlin«, summen Sie vor sich hin, beim Spaziergang über den Hackeschen Markt, beim Blick vom Fernsehturm hinunter auf die Stadt oder beim Besuch der Museumsinsel. Stimmt ja auch.

Doch Berlin ist viel mehr. Und dieses Mehr finden Sie nicht Unter den Linden, nicht im Lichterglanz des Kurfürstendamms, in keiner Arkade, in keinem der unzähligen Center. Aber direkt dahinter: am Rand des Geschehens, im Schatten der Scheinwerfer, im Rücken der Stadt.

Dieses Buch führt Sie in den Backstage-Bereich der Hauptstadt, hinter die Bühne, dort wo Groupies auf ihren Star warten, der verschwitzt, aber erleichtert hinter den Vorhang tritt. Und hier, im fahlen Licht der Kulisse, eben genau so aussieht, wie er ist. Das ist ein Moment der Begeisterung und der Enttäuschung: Nie waren Sie Ihrem Star näher, doch so gut wie auf der Bühne bewegt er sich dahinter nicht …

»Backstage Berlin« ist eine Hommage an Orte und Menschen, die für sich mit dem gleichen Recht behaupten können, Berlin zu sein, wie Fernsehturm, Olympiastadion & Co. Hier, auf der Rückseite, führen bislang keine »Guides« vorbei, kein Fremdenführer zeigt die Stadt hinter dem Vorhang, mit ihren tiefen Narben, ehrlichen Farben und dieser herrlichen Tristesse.

*Markus C. Hurek*

ALEXAND PLATZ

Of course you know the Reichstag, the Brandenburg Gate and Knut the polar bear. »That's Berlin«, you tell yourself as you stroll across Hackescher Markt, ride the elevator up the TV tower or visit Museum Island. And you're not wrong.

But there is much more to Berlin than that. Much more that you won't find on Unter den Linden. Nor beneath the bright lights of Kurfürstendamm, in shopping arcades and the countless newly built complexes. But look behind them and next to them: on the margins, in the shadows cast by the floodlights, behind the city's back.

This book takes you backstage in Germany's capital city, behind the scenes where the groupies are waiting for their star, who steps behind the curtain, covered in sweat but feeling relieved. And here, in the wan light of the stage set, you see him as he really is. This is a moment for rapture and disappointment: you never got so close to your hero, but backstage he doesn't move the way he does up front …

»Backstage Berlin« is a tribute to people and places who have just as much right as the TV tower, the Olympic stadium and all the rest to say »we are what makes Berlin«. Here, round the back, is where no guides come, and no-one shows tourists what lies behind the curtain: the city of deep scars, honest colours and a magnificent sadness.

*Markus C. Hurek*

Arminiusstraße, Moabit

# »Berlin war ein Fest, ein Wirbelsturm, eine Revolution!«

Claire Goll

»Berlin was a celebration, a whirlwind, a revolution!«

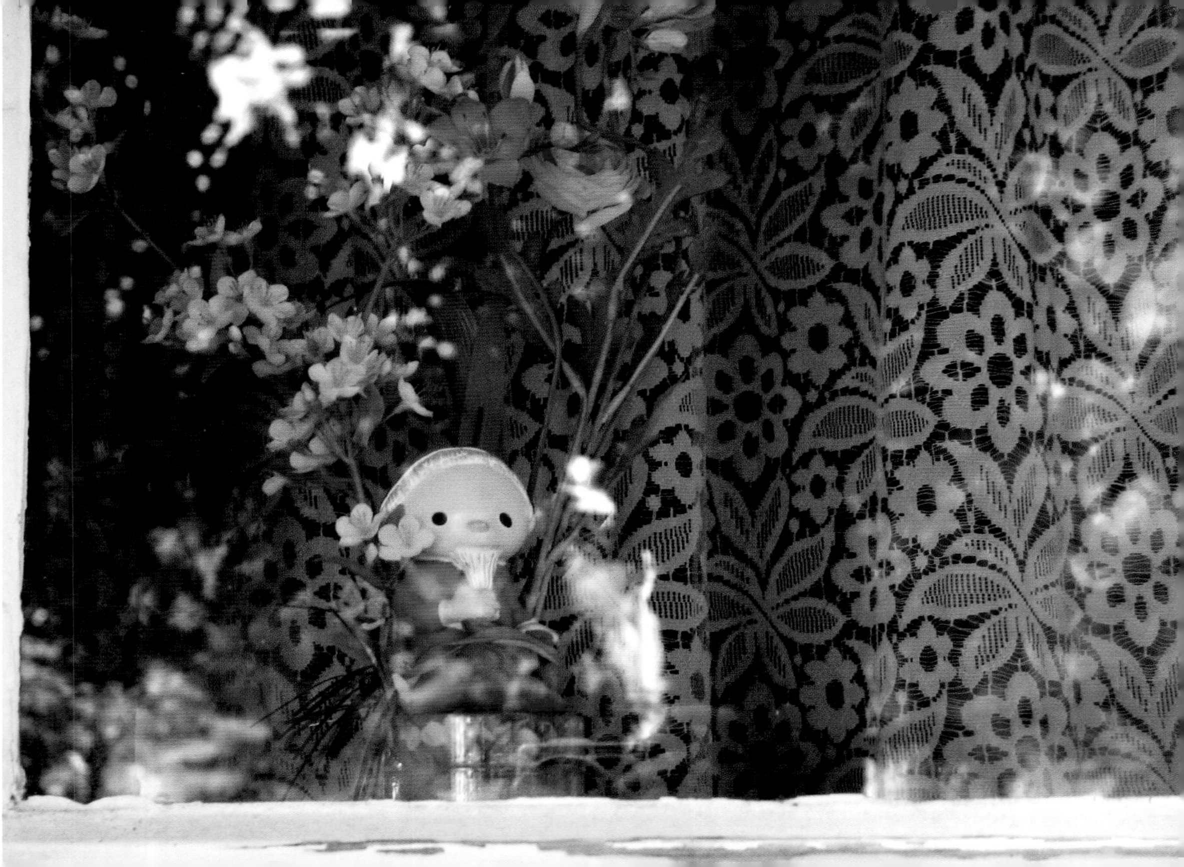

Egmontstraße, Rummelsburg

Tucholskystraße, Mitte

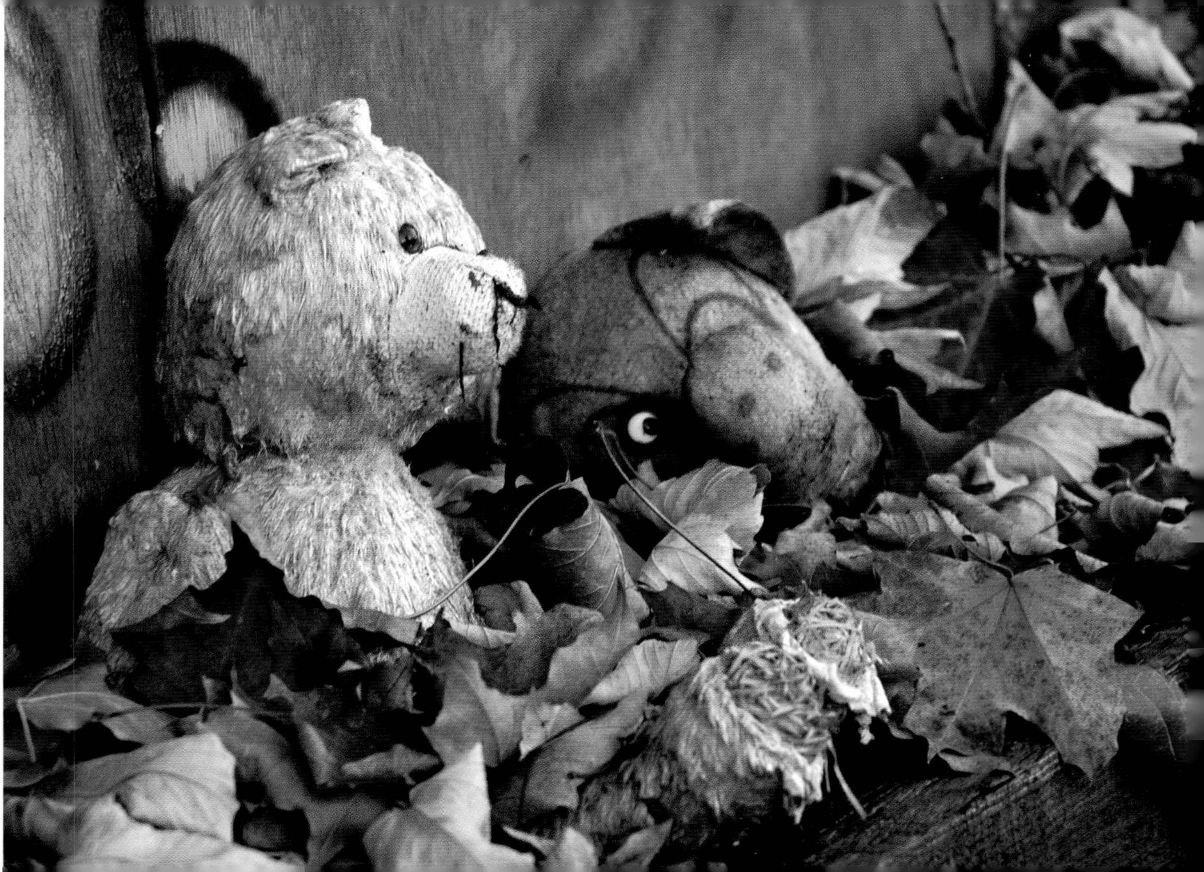

Mauerpark, Prenzlauer Berg

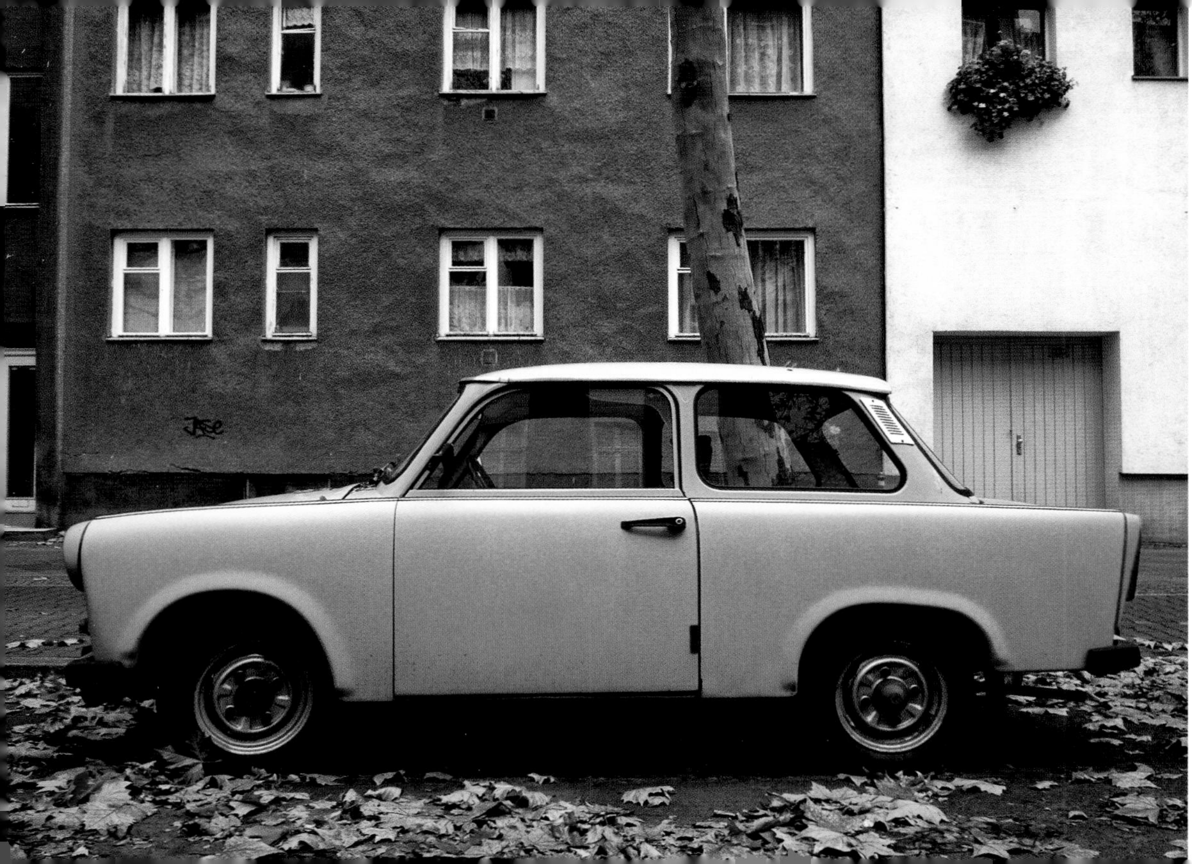

Obentrautstraße, Kreuzberg

Düsseldorfer Straße, Wilmersdorf | Heckerdamm, Charlottenburg

Düsseldorfer Straße, Wilmersdorf

Mit lieben letzten Grüßen

HEINO und Hannelore

Kurfürstenstraße, Tiergarten

# »Berlin ist arm, aber **sexy** !«

Klaus Wowereit

»Berlin is poor, but sexy!«

sloggi®

Locker bleiben, Jungs!

Hardenbergstraße, Charlottenburg

Café Bar COMEIN

zu vermieten
0 88 56 21-0

Zutritt für
Jugendliche
unter 18 Jahren
verboten!

Alt-Moabit, Moabit

JUDY'S KINO-BAR

MO–FR 12⁰⁰–2⁰⁰  SA 18⁰⁰–?

Kirchhofstraße, Rixdorf

Paschas
Harem

WELLNESS
SAUNA
CLUB
GROSSBILDLEINWAND

Willkommen!

EROTISCHES
MUSIKCAFÉ
AUF ÜBER 350 m²

GIRLS

Beusselstraße, Moabit

Mauerpark, Prenzlauer Berg | Klausingring, Charlottenburg

PIGALLE bar PIGALLE bar

Sanderstraße, Neukölln

Dominicusstraße, Schöneberg

Ebertstraße, Tiergarten

**Revaler Straße, Friedrichshain**

»Auf Schritt und Tritt
fehlt mir jetzt
die wohltuende Gemütlichkeit
und Kultur der Schweiz.
Und auch
die **Reinlichkeit**.«

Rosa Luxemburg

»At every step I miss the comforting cosiness and culture of Switzerland. As well as its cleanliness.«

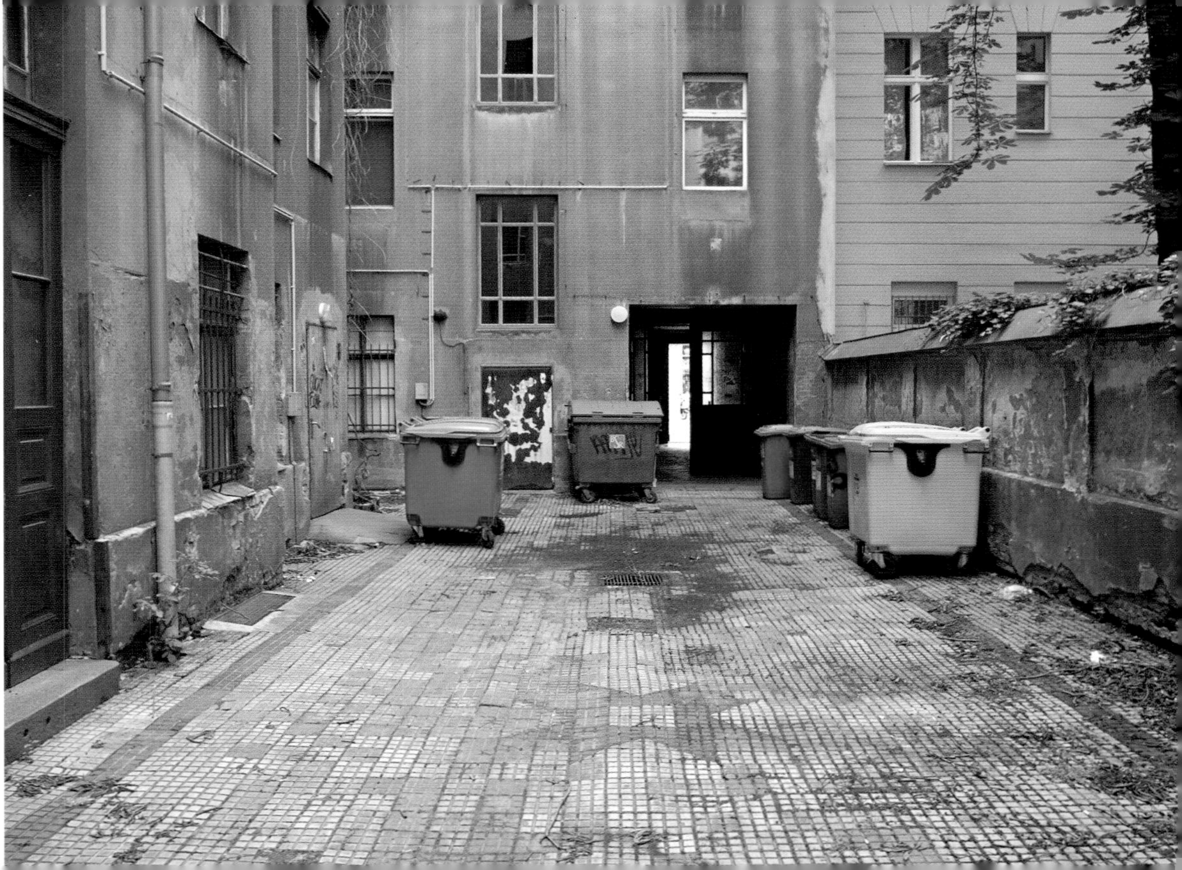

Kastanienallee, Prenzlauer Berg

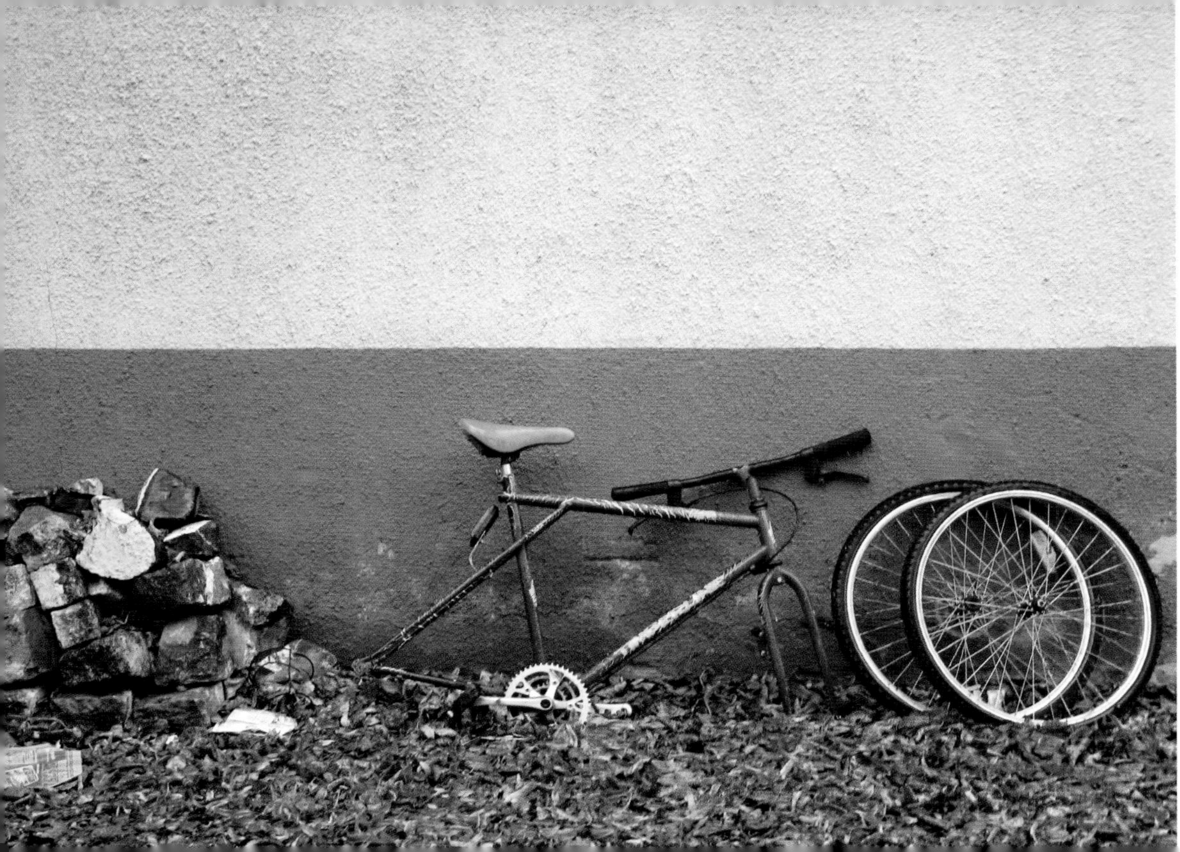

Stromstraße, Moabit

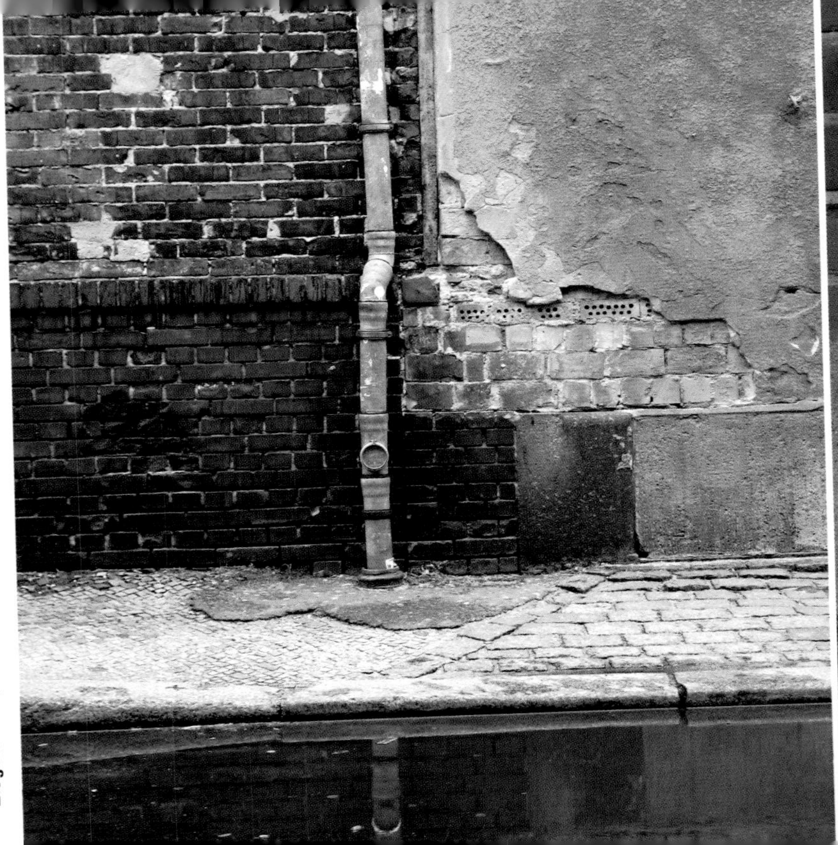

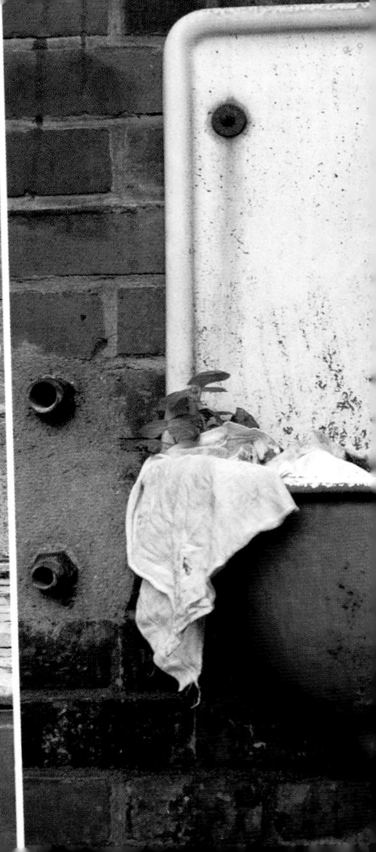

Ziegelstraße, Mitte | Ritterstraße, Kreuzberg

Lebuser Straße, Friedrichshain

Liebe Gäste!
Wir bitten Sie bei Benutzung
des Parkplatzes laute Gespräche
laute Motorengeräusche
sowie Türenschlagen zu ver-
meiden
Ihr
Rosario
Steakhaus

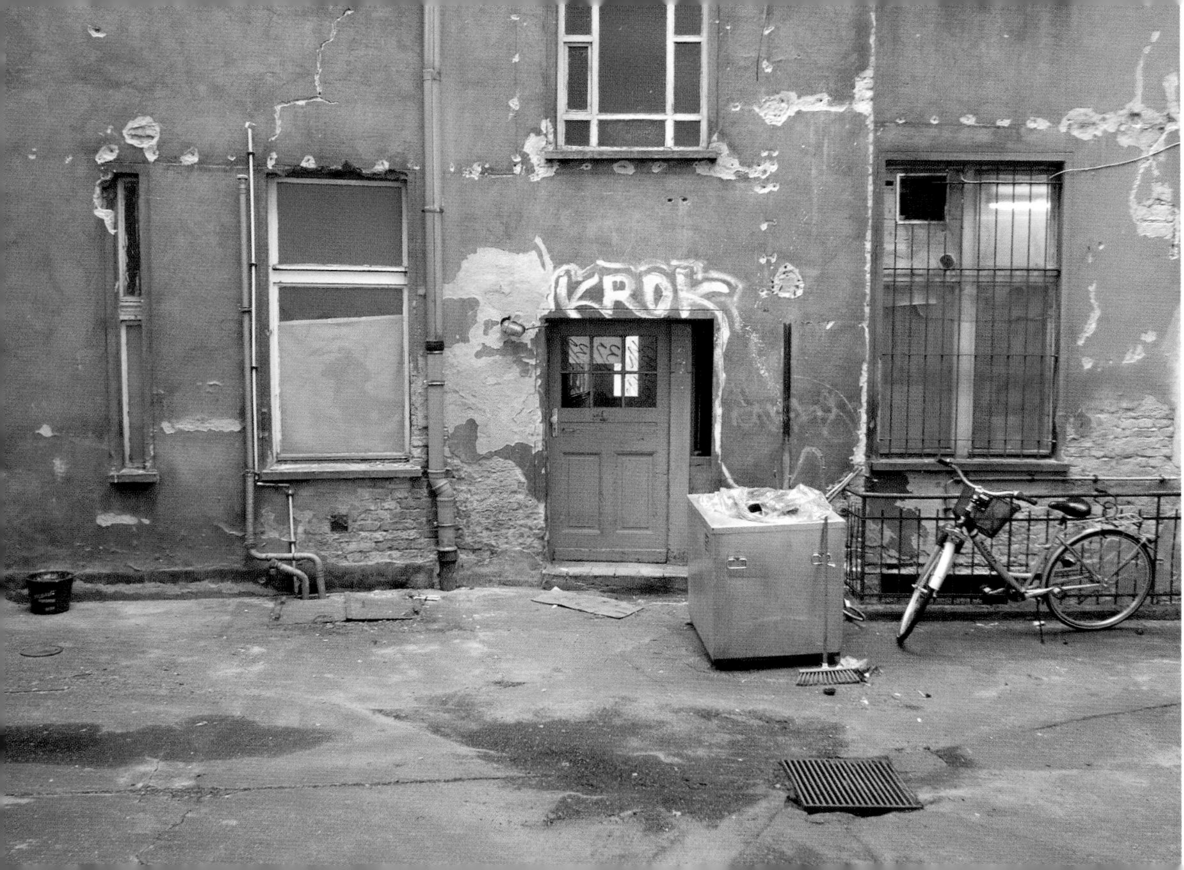


Simon-Dach-Straße, Friedrichshain

Marktstraße, Reinickendorf

Pallasstraße, Schöneberg

»Das Grausenerregende,
Schreckliche wird gewagt:
**Wohnen** in Berlin.«

Karl Gutzkow (1869)

»A spine-chilling, horrifying adventure: living in Berlin.«

Gute Aussichten
und ideales
Wohnen

BAUGENOSSENSCHAFT
IDEAL

120

Fritz-Erler-Allee, Gropiusstadt

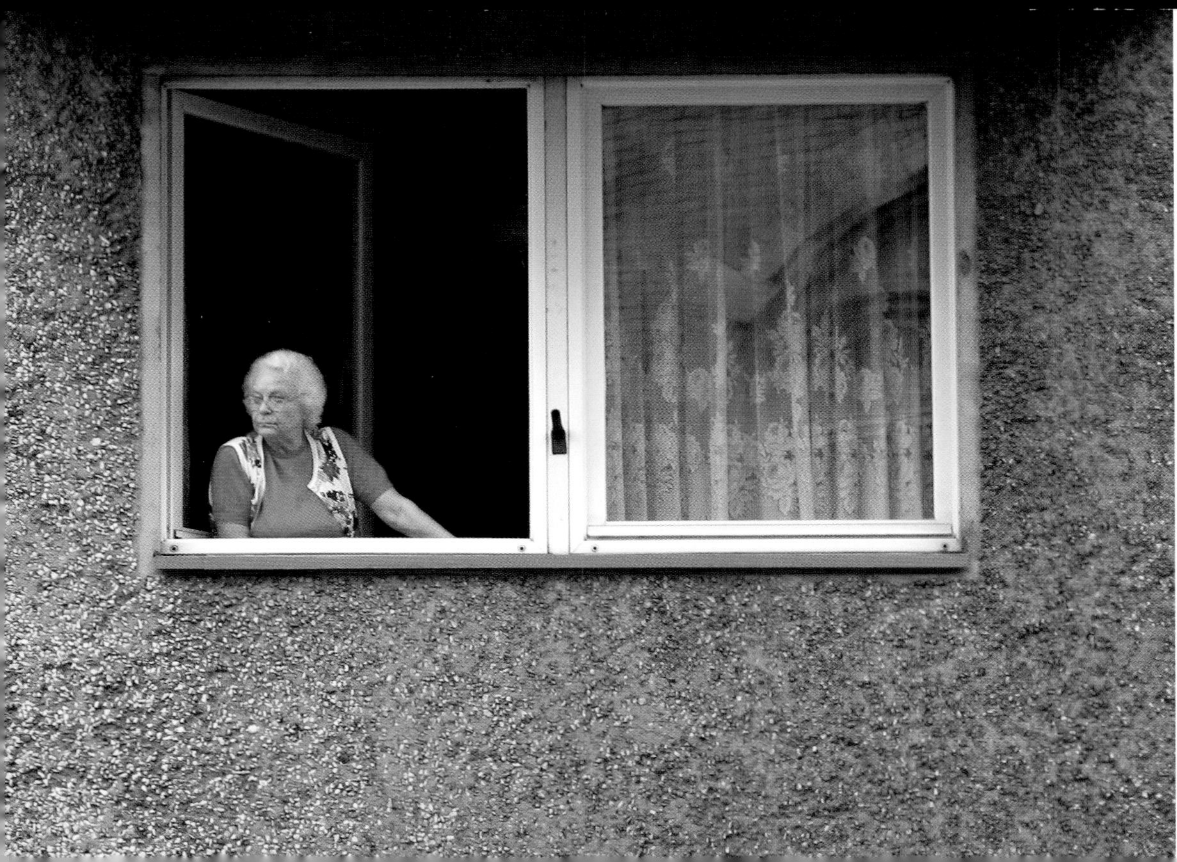

Münzstraße, Mitte

Geschützte Grünanlage

GESETZ VOM 3. 11. 1962

Rostocker Straße, Wedding
Gerviniusstraße, Charlottenburg

Düsseldorfer Straße, Wilmersdorf
Hoeppnerstraße, Tempelhof

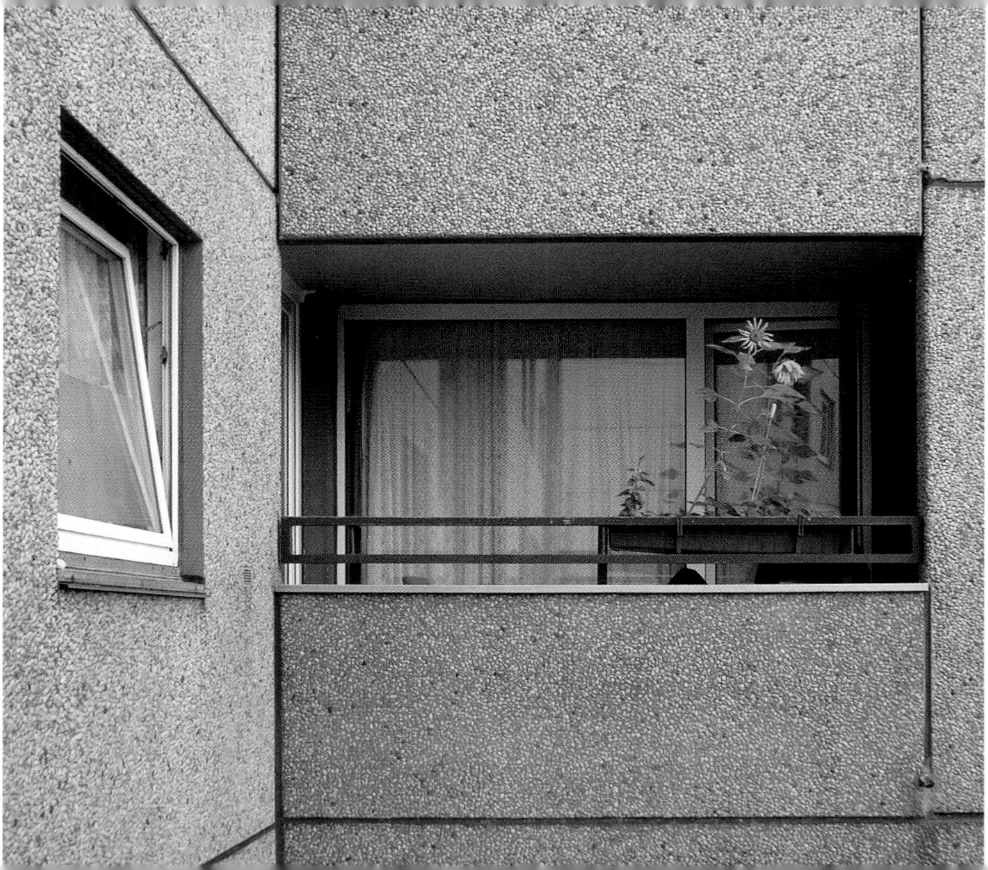

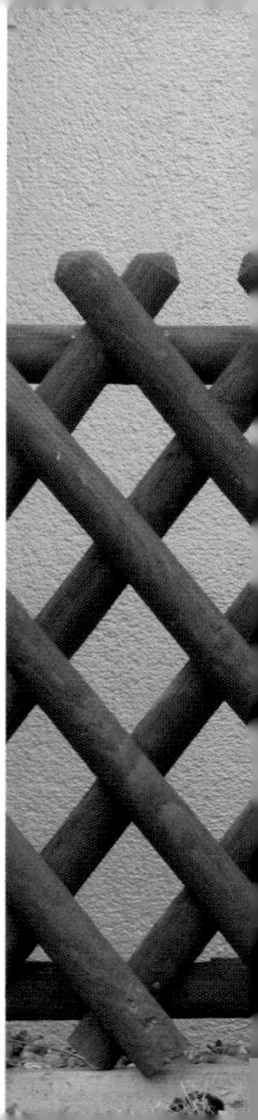

Bergfriedstraße, Kreuzberg | Heckerdamm, Charlottenburg

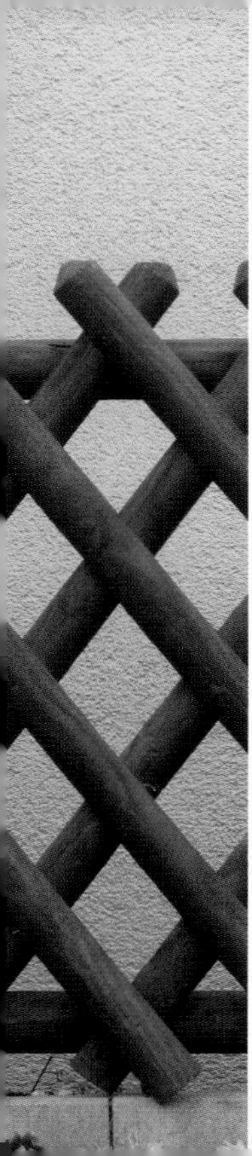
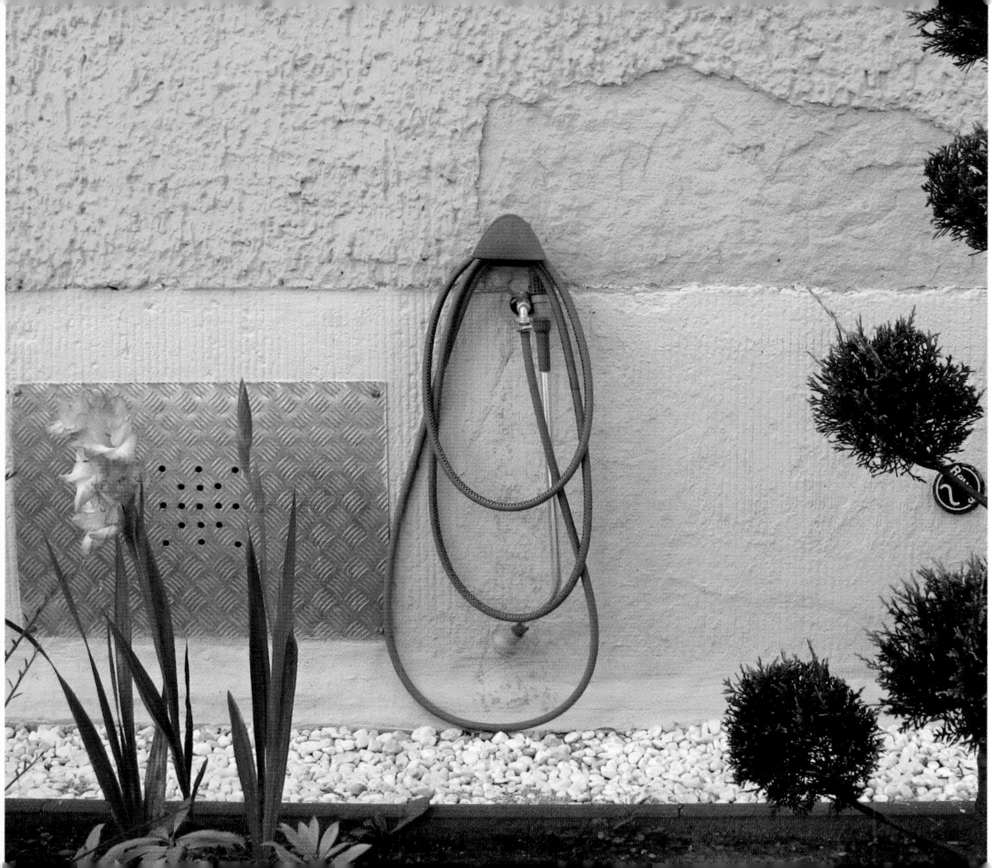

Türrschmidtstraße, Rummelsburg

Hardenbergstraße, Charlottenburg

»Man muss, wie so oft,
das Leben der Stadt
von den **Inschriften**
ablesen.«

Franz Hessel

»As so often, you have to read the life of the city from the inscriptions.«

Uhlandstraße, Wilmersdorf

EIER WALKOK

P
WALKOK

Quedlinburger Straße, Charlottenburg

Café

WC

Außer
LKW
UND
Mieter

Müllhaus

Grunewaldstraße, Schöneberg

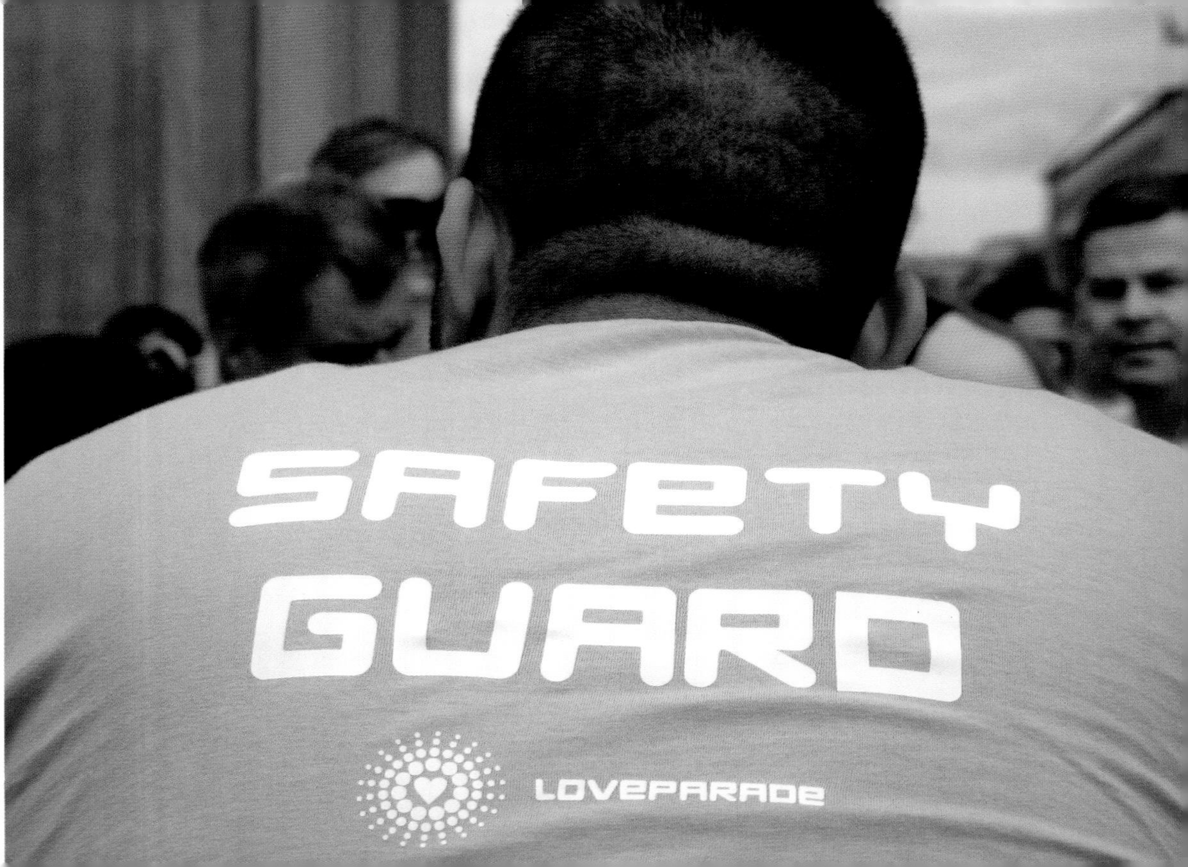


Platz des 18. März, Tiergarten

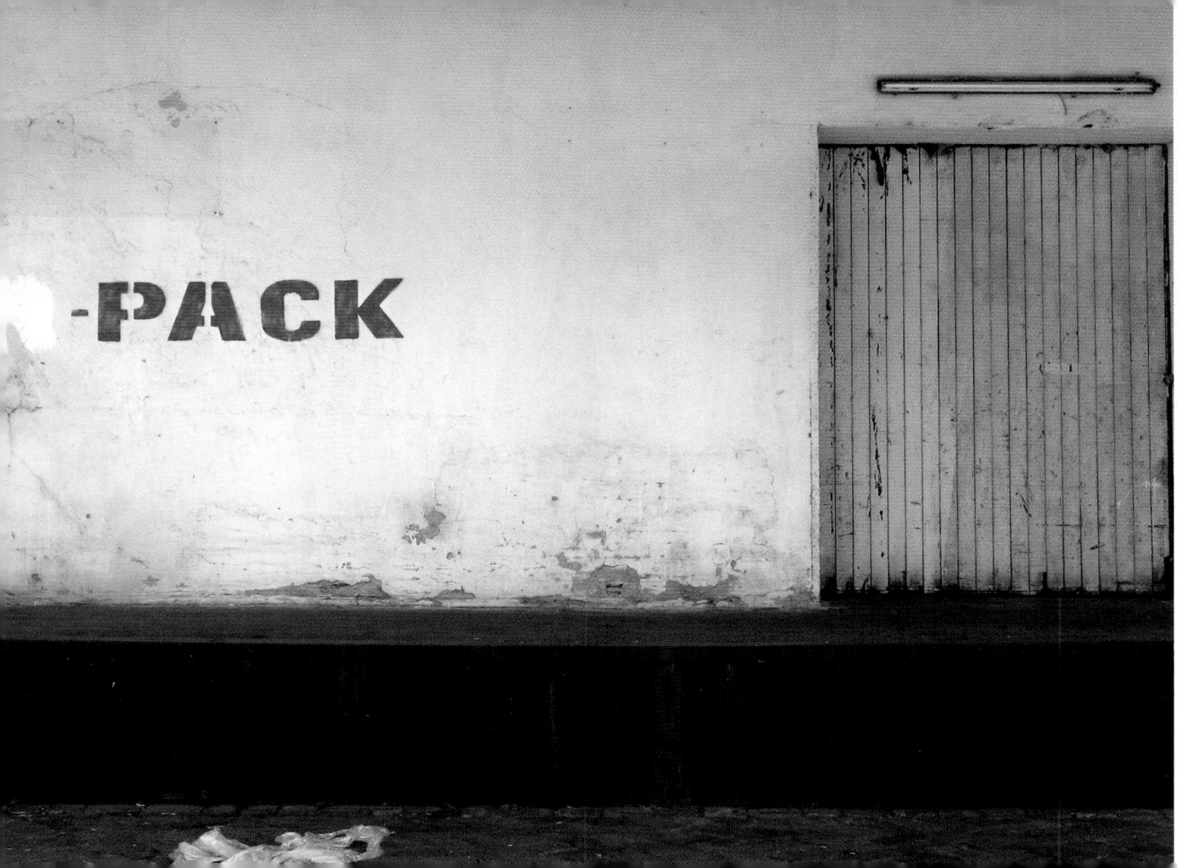


Heidestraße, Tiergarten

**Körnerstraße, Tiergarten**

»Mein Gott, was für eine **langweilige,** entsetzliche Stadt ist Berlin!«

Fjodor M. Dostojewski (1874)

»My God, what a boring, dreadful city Berlin is!«

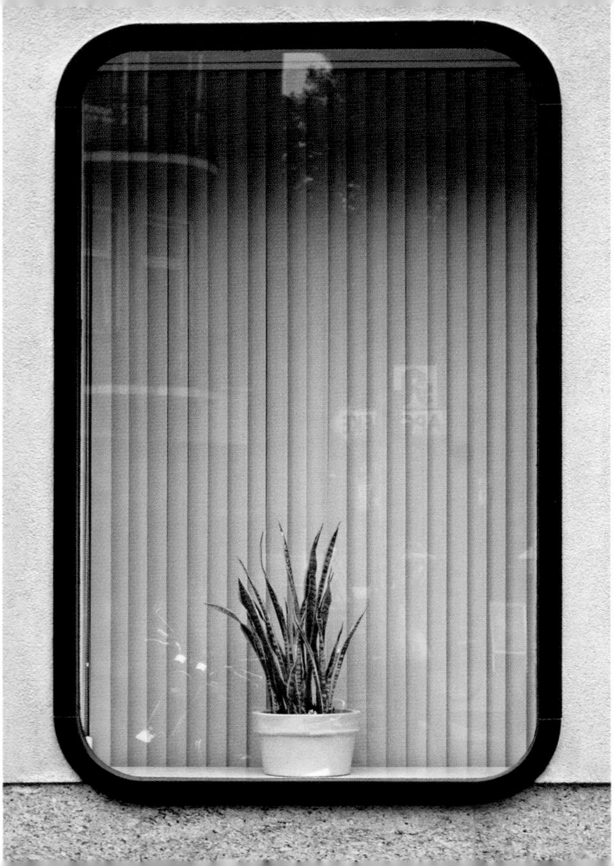

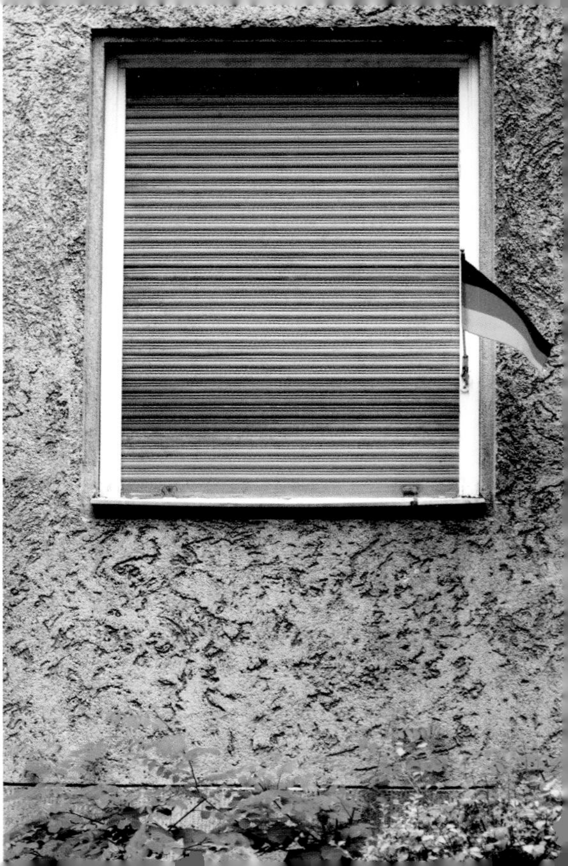

Uhlandstraße, Wilmersdorf | Plöner Straße, Schmargendorf

Linienstraße, Mitte | Sansibarstraße, Wedding

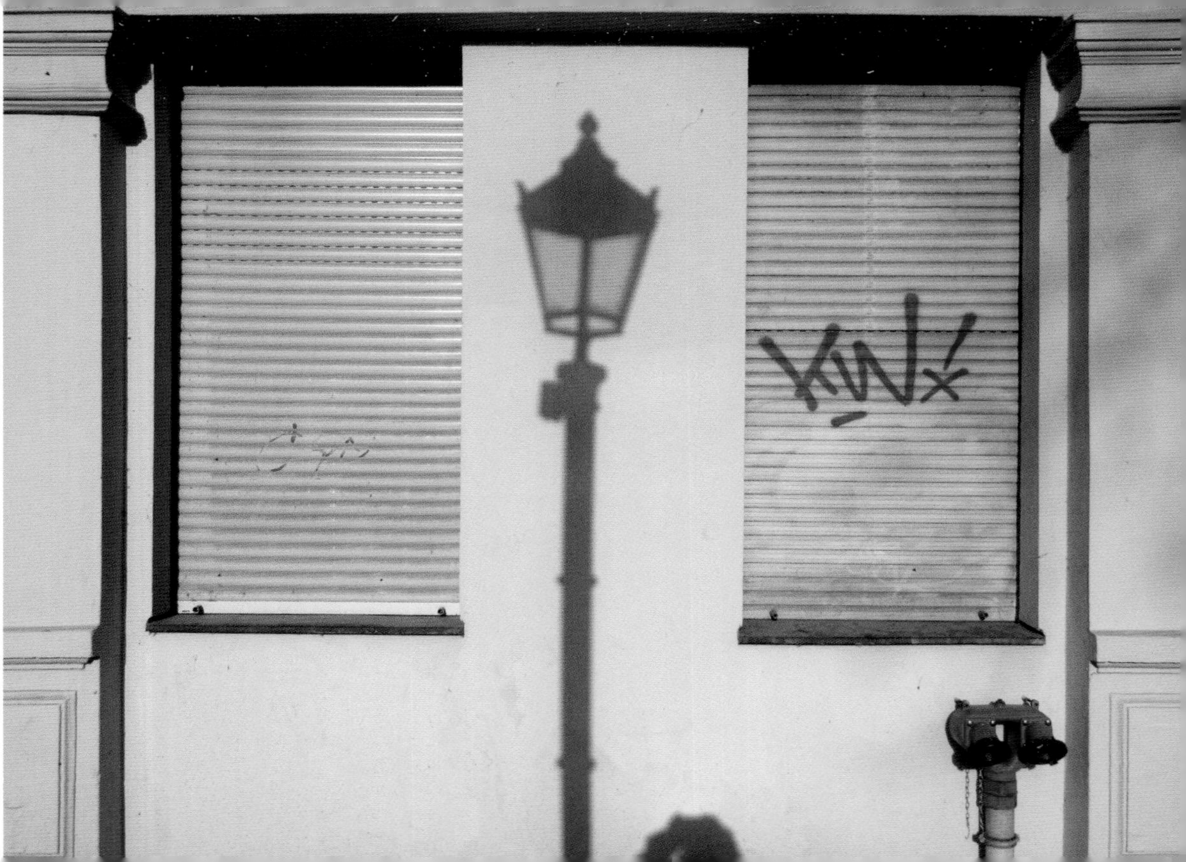

Fraenkelufer, Kreuzberg

Sanderstraße, Neukölln | Sansibarstraße, Wedding

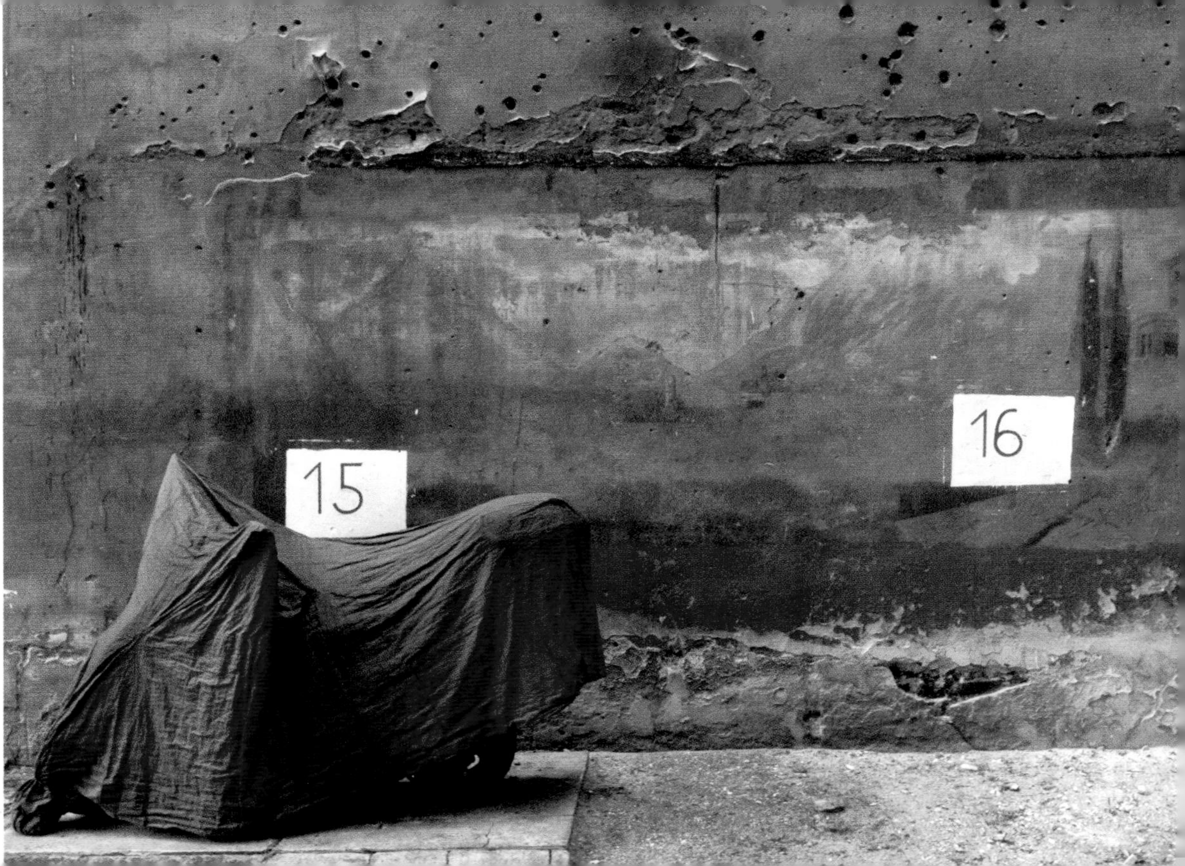

Werftstraße, Moabit

Lüderitzstraße, Wedding

**Altonaer Straße, Hansaviertel**

# »In der **Küche** des Berliners passiert selten viel.«

**Jakob Hein** *(Gebrauchsanweisung für Berlin, 2006)*

»Normally not much happens in a Berliner's kitchen.«

WURST :)

| Frische | | Bockwurst | |
|---|---|---|---|
| Pommes Frites | 1,70 | im Brötchen | 2,10 |
| hausgem. vom Ketchup | | Currywurst | |
| o. andere Soßen | 0,30 | mit Brötchen | 2,10 |
| scharfe Zwiebeln | 0,50 | | |
| | | Bratwurst | 2,30 |
| Kaffee | 1,00/1,50 | im Brötchen | |
| Tee | 1,00 | | |
| Kakao | 2,00 | Backwurst | 2,20 |
| Getränke | 1,50/2,00 | mit Brötchen | |
| Bier, Bio Weisse | 2,00 | scharfe | |
| | | Zwiebeln | 0,50 |

Ebertstraße, Tiergarten

Amsterdamer Straße, Wedding | Großbeerenstraße, Kreuzberg | Münzstraße, Mitte

Fehrbelliner Platz, Wilmersdorf | Hoeppnerstraße, Tempelhof

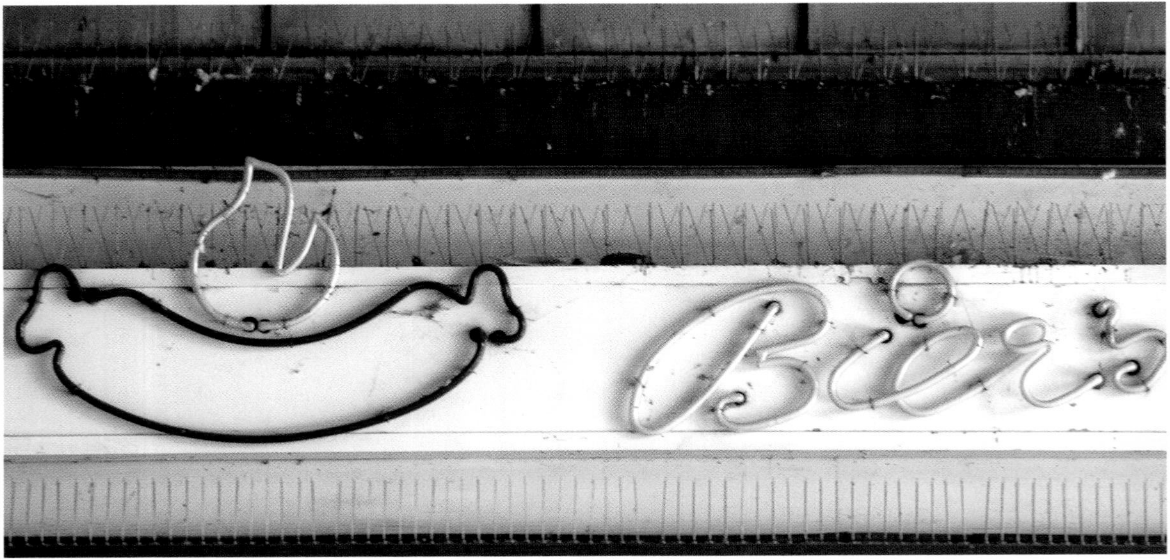

Friedrichstraße, Mitte

Mehringdamm, Kreuzberg
Breitscheidplatz, Charlottenburg

Fehrbelliner Platz, Wilmersdorf
Eberswalder Straße, Prenzlauer Berg

**Potsdamer Platz, Tiergarten**

# »Berlin, nun **freue** Dich!«

Walter Momper (1989)

»Berlin, rejoice now!«

Zoologischer Garten, Charlottenburg

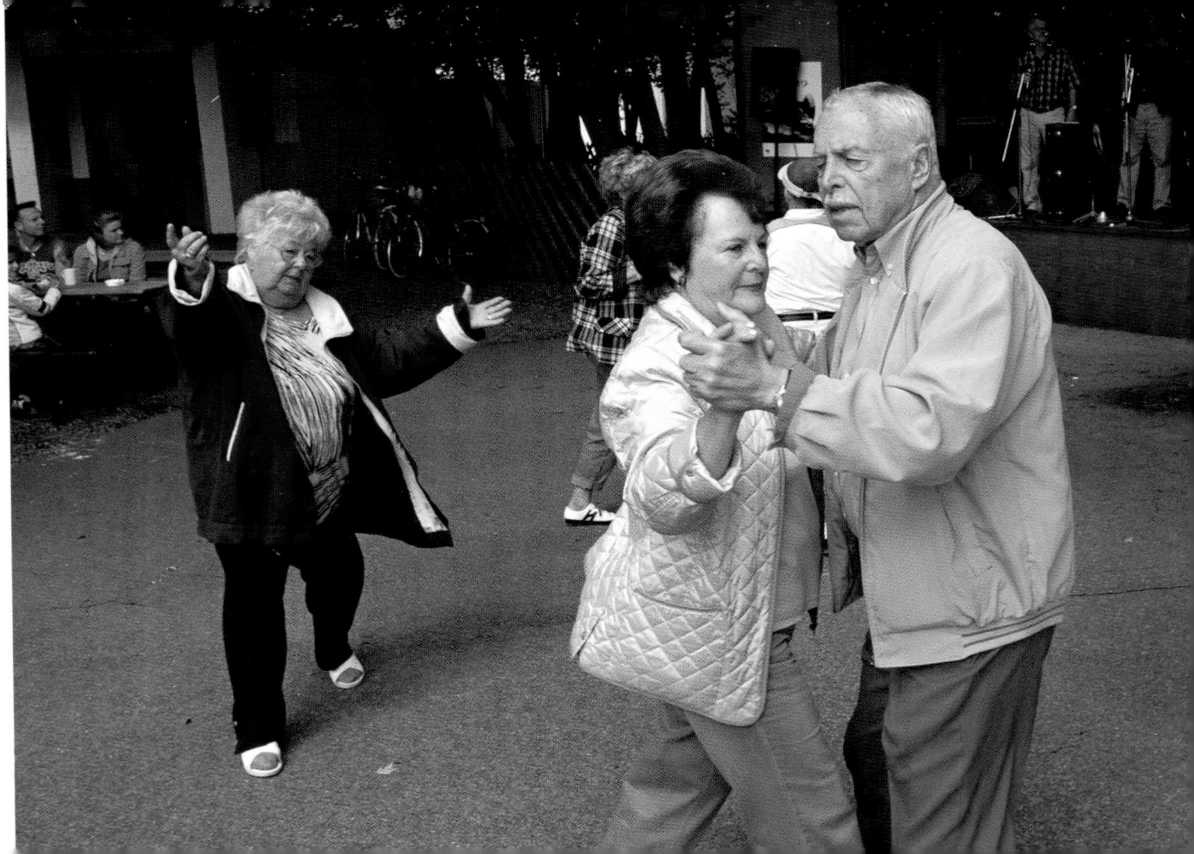

Plänterwald, Treptow

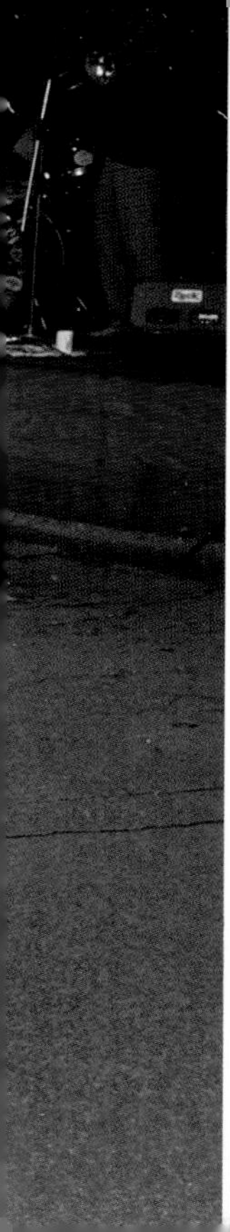

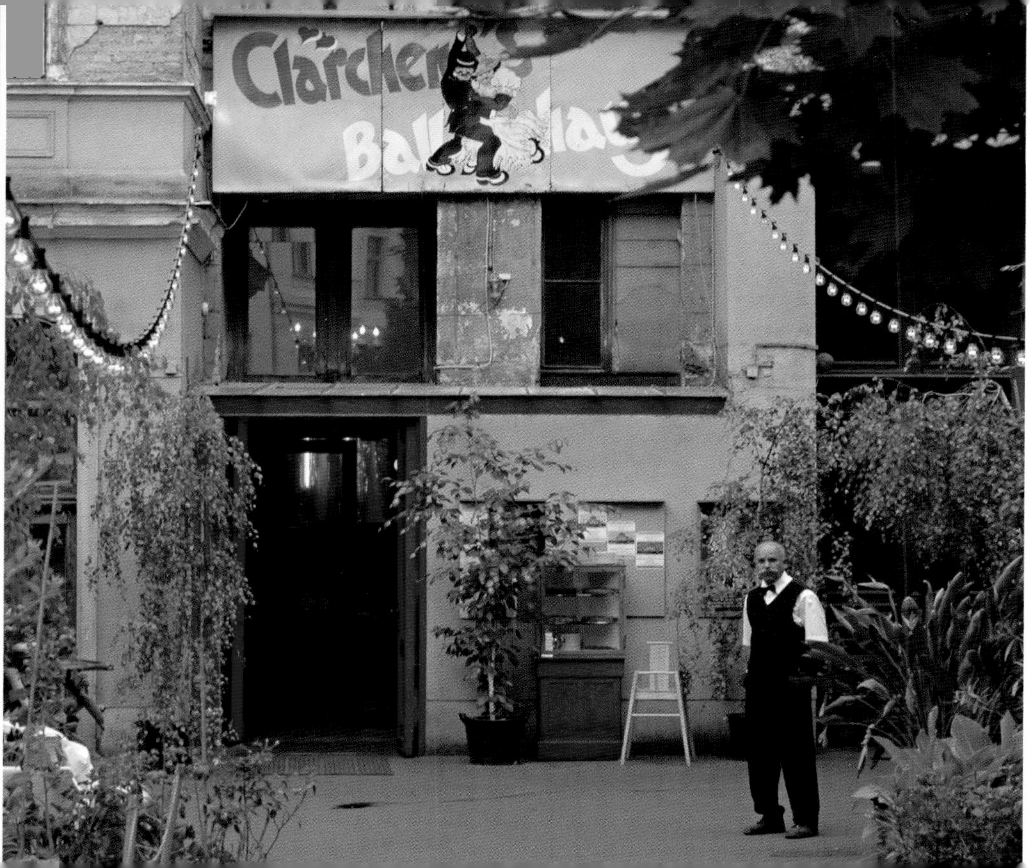

Auguststraße, Mitte

**Lila, Charlottenburg**

»be **Berlin**!«

Stadtmarketing

»be Berlin!«

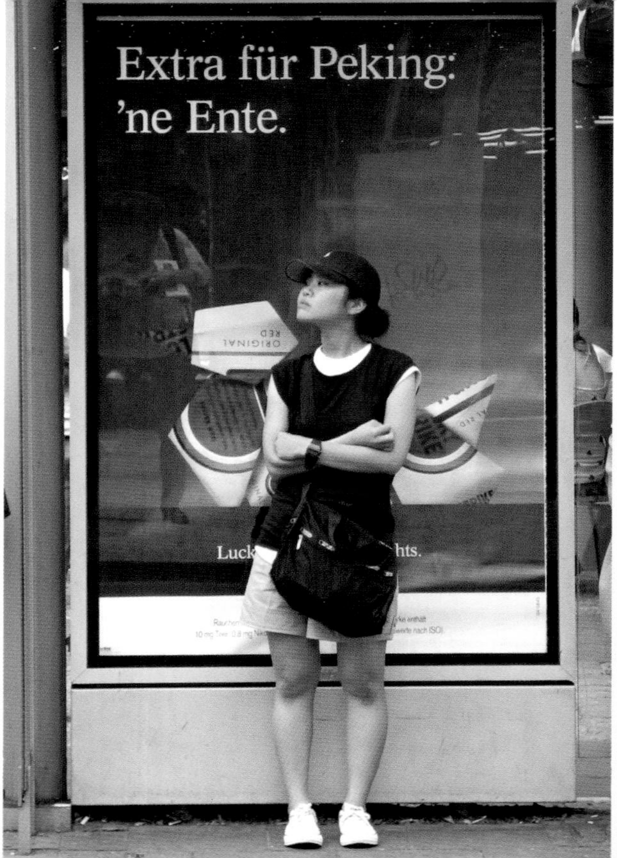

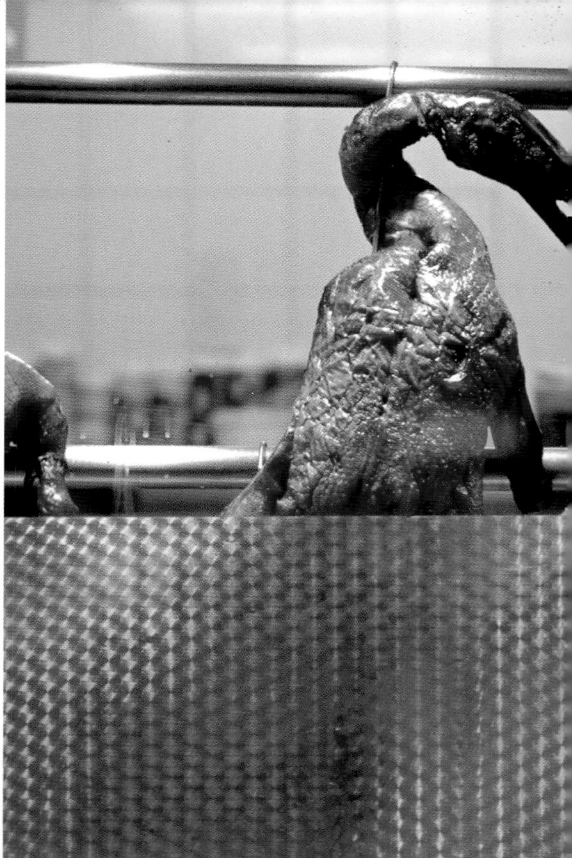

Potsdamer Straße, Tiergarten

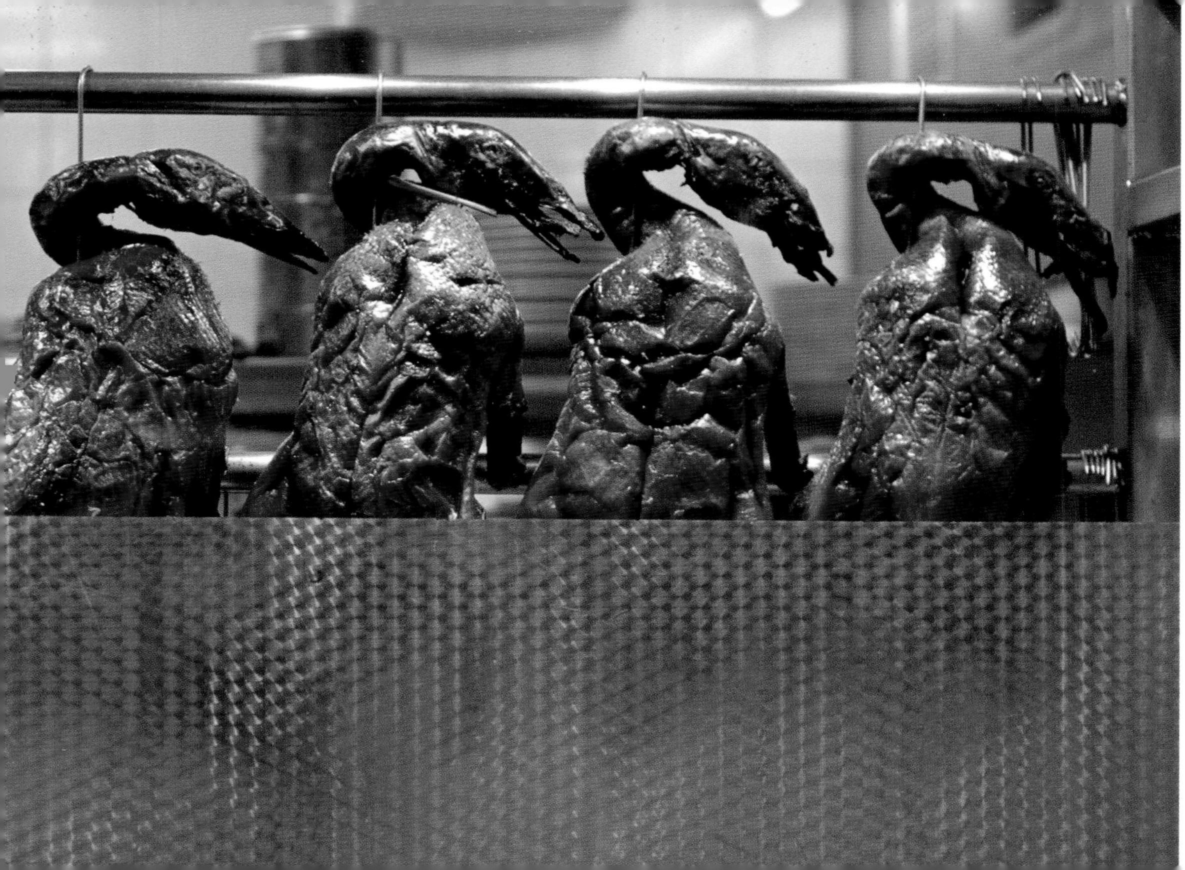

Kantstraße, Charlottenburg

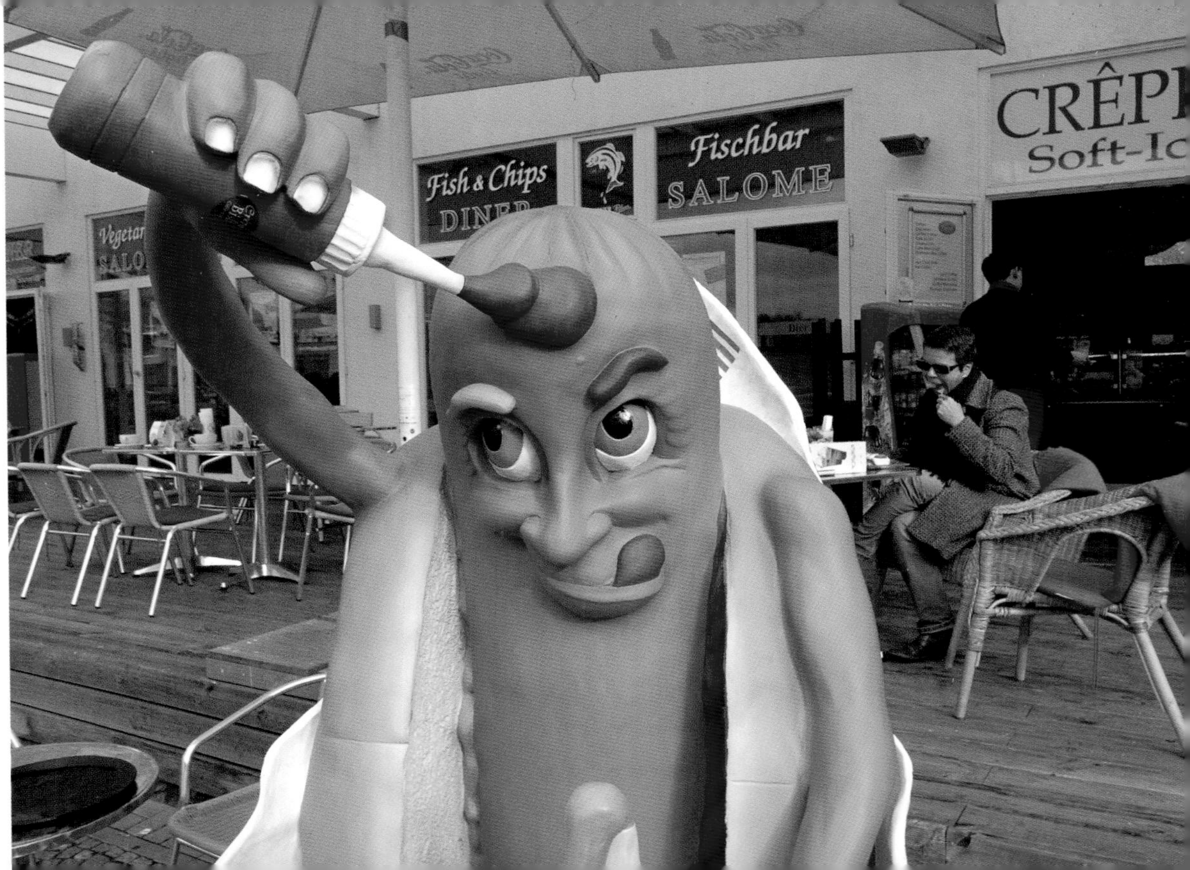


Cora-Berliner-Straße, Mitte

»Ich fühle mich hier ein
bisschen wie in Südfrankreich.
Ich habe immer das Gefühl,
ich müsste gleich an den
**Strand** gehen.«

Herbert Grönemeyer

»Here I feel a little bit like in the south of France.
I always have the feeling that it's time to go down to the beach.«

© Prestel Verlag
Munich · Berlin · London · New York, 2009

Umschlag / Cover
Vorderseite / Front: Oranienburger Straße, Mitte
Rückseite / Back: Tempelhofer Damm, Tempelhof

Die Deutsche Bibliothek verzeichnet diese Publikation in der Deutschen
Nationalbibliografie; detaillierte bibliografische Angaben sind im
Internet über http://dnb.ddb.de abrufbar

Die Deutsche Bibliothek lists this publication in the Deutsche
Nationalbibliografie; detailed bibliographic data is available on the
Internet at http://dnb.ddb.de

The Library of Congress Cataloguing-in-Publication data is available.

Prestel Verlag
Königinstraße 9
D-80539 München
Tel. +49 (89) 24 29 08-300
Fax +49 (89) 24 29 08-335
info@prestel.de

Prestel Büro Berlin
Husemannstraße 26
D-10435 Berlin
Tel. +49 (30) 425 01 85
Fax +49 (30) 425 01 85
www.prestel.de

Prestel Publishing Ltd.
4 Bloomsbury Place · London WC1A 2QA
Tel. +44 (0)20 7323-5004
Fax +44 (0)20 7636-8004

Prestel Publishing
900 Broadway, Suite 603 New York, NY 10003
Tel. +1 (212) 995-2720
Fax +1 (212) 995-2733
www.prestel.com

Prestel books are available worldwide.

Please contact your nearest bookseller or write to one of the above
addresses for information concerning your local distributor.

Übersetzung / Translation: John Sykes, Cologne
Lektorat / Editor: Frauke Berchtig
Copy-editing by Curt Holtz
Gestaltung / Design: Kerstin Schröer, Berlin
Herstellung / Layout: Astrid Wedemeyer
Reproduktion / Origination: Reproline Mediateam Achter, München
Druck und Bindung / Printing and binding: TBB, Banská Bystrica

Gedruckt in der Slowakischen Republik
auf chlorfrei gebleichtem Papier / Printed in Slovakia on acid-free paper

ISBN 978-3-7913-4187-3

Fotonachweis / Photographic Credits
Alle Aufnahmen entstanden von 2006 bis 2008 und stammen von /
All photographs were taken between 2006 and 2008 by
© Markus C. Hurek, Potsdam